One More Bug

Bug

An Insect Addition Book

by Martha E. H. Rustad

AMICUS READERS 1 AMICUS INK

amicus readers

Say Hello to Amicus Readers.

You'll find our helpful dog, Amicus, chasing a ball—to let you know the reading level of a book.

1
Learn to Read
High frequency words and close photo-text matches introduce familiar topics and provide ample support for brand new readers.

2
Read Independently
Some repetition is mixed with varied sentence structures and a select amount of new vocabulary words are introduced with text and photo support.

3
Read to Know More
Interesting facts and engaging art and photos give fluent readers fun books both for reading practice and to learn about new topics.

Amicus Readers and Amicus Ink are imprints of Amicus
P.O. Box 1329, Mankato, MN 56002
www.amicuspublishing.us

Library of Congress Cataloging-in-Publication Data
Names: Rustad, Martha E. H. (Martha Elizabeth Hillman), 1975- author.
Title: One more bug : an insect addition book / by Martha E. H. Rustad.
Description: Mankato, MN : Amicus, [2017] | Series: 1, 2, 3 count with me | Audience: K to grade 3.
Identifiers: LCCN 2015040336 | ISBN 9781607539230 (library binding) ISBN 9781681521145 (pbk.) | ISBN 9781681510477 (ebk.)
Subjects: LCSH: Addition--Juvenile literature. | Insects--Juvenile literature.
Classification: LCC QA115 .R76 2017 | DDC 513.2/11--dc23
LC record available at http://lccn.loc.gov/2015040336

Photo Credits: All photos from iStock except: Corbis/Roger Tidman, 7, 24; Shutterstock/Marco Uliana, cover; Shutterstock/Eric Isselee/12-13; Superstock/agefotostock, 1; Superstock/Animals Animals, 3, Superstock/Biosphoto, 4

Editor   Rebecca Glaser
Designer   Tracy Myers

Printed in the United States of America

HC 10 9 8 7 6 5 4 3 2 1
PB 10 9 8 7 6 5 4 3 2 1

Let's look for insects.

I see one, two, three!

How many more will we find?

1+1=2

One bumblebee buzzes to a flower. One more follows. Now two bumblebees are collecting pollen.

2+1=3

Two ladybugs sit.

One more ladybug joins.

Three ladybugs eat aphids.

8

2+2=4

Two walking sticks hide on a tree. Two more walking sticks come along. Four walking sticks use camouflage to stay safe.

2 + 3 = 5

Two dragonflies rest. Three more dragonflies swoop down. Five dragonflies rest in the garden.

5+1=6

Five praying mantises turn their heads. One praying mantis catches a bug. Six praying mantises have strong jaws.

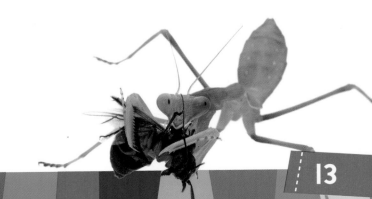

5+2=7

Five flies gather at a picnic.

Two more flies come over.

Seven flies suck up food.

15

7+1=8

Seven water striders sit on a pond. One more joins them. Eight water striders move across the water.

Eight moths flutter to a light. One more comes. Nine moths fly around the lantern.

$$8+1=9$$

5+5=10

Five wasps sit on a paper
nest. Five more buzz nearby.
Ten wasps make this nest
bigger.

Ten ants walk in a line.

One more ant joins them.

Eleven ants crawl into their anthill.

Can you count all the insects?

10+1=11

Add Again

Add the number of objects in each box.

2+3

5+4

1+2

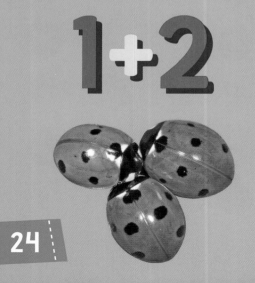

4+3